Step Forward in Solidarity

*Poems gathered in celebration
of International Women's Day 2025*

Published 2025 by Earthy Little Acorns Poetry Press
Station Road, Billingshurst, West Sussex, England.

Copyright © remains with individual poets: Liz Barnes, Kate Collier, Nicola Garrard and Ted Gooda, in accordance with Section 77 of the Copyright, Designs and Patents Act 1988.

All rights reserved. No part of this publication may be reproduced, stored in or introduced into a retrieval system, or transmitted, in any form, or by any means (electronic, mechanical, photocopying, recording or otherwise) without the prior written permission of the publisher. Any person who does any unauthorised act in relation to this publication may be liable to criminal prosecution and civil claims for damages.

Printed and bound by JR Print, Horsham

A CIP catalogue record for this book is available from the British Library

ISBN number: 978-1-0687570-2-0

Cover artwork by Liz Barnes

CONTENTS

- I. AWARENESS OF OTHERNESS
  The difference between boys and girls 1
  A Hundred Vaginas of Solitude 2
  My Friend Sharon 4

- II. WARY OF OTHERS
  Could a woman have an ego like this? 5
  Virginia 6
  Stepping stone 8
  The Ringmaster 9
  Do you love me? 10

- III. MATERNAL AWARENESS
  Wish you were here 12
  Little bedtime story 13
  A plea to the Young Unloved Mother 14

- IV. BE AWARE
  Pink 15
  Birth day 16
  Cot poems 18

- V. BEWARE
  Birch syrup 19
  Breast work 20
  What a shame 21
  Banishing the branks 22
  Step forward in solidarity 24

I. AWARENESS OF OTHERNESS

The difference between boys and girls

I'm only five when I'm asked if I know
the difference between boys and girls.
I do, of course: girls wear tights.
Wretched things, all encasing, wrinkled,
twisted up, wrong-way-round heels,
something lumpy but unreachable
near the toes. Or falling down,
sweaty, stretchy, saggy crotch-drop.

Later, the teenage slagginess
of a ladder, lacing up the thigh.
A hole in your hosiery.
If only the tyranny of tights
was the worst of it.
But oh, when you worked at it until
you felt the satisfying rip
of destruction, and release.

Ted Gooda

I. AWARENESS OF OTHERNESS

A Hundred Vaginas of Solitude
- a tribute to Laura Dodsworth
& Gabriel Garcia Márquez

Here's one from a while ago
A documentary
of a woman photographer
who offers a hundred women
a photo of their vaginas
-Vulvas actually
So they can see their beauty.
100 vaginas on TV
something for all women to see
free from pornography.

It seems a woman's anatomy
still holds greater secrecy
doesn't hold a man's
outward transparency
Isn't it true even today
There's little conversation
or even a mention of
clitoral sensations.
Not the attention of
men's erections, penetration,
ejaculation
and - erectile dysfunction.
Can you imagine a teenage boy
not knowing his rising cock?
The very stock and size
which constantly takes him
by surprise.

But there's many a girl
that can only trace
the contours of her labia
her unseen genitalia
really can't tell
picture what it is
that makes her tingle and reach below.
Our vaginas that belong to us
seen briefly by others, lovers in
foreplay
lie unseen, stowed away, even today
Except in textbook diagrams
lessons in human biology -
it's still suppressed
by that Victorian history
remaining deep in our psyche.

After all for many women
what she held below
that strange-shaped fishy mystery
was something she really
didn't want to know
because it carried
the chance of pregnancy.
The blame and the shame
the indignity
being chained to a man
to save your name
or finding some place
in the backstreet somewhere
with trembling, danger and fear.

I. AWARENESS OF OTHERNESS

So this unseen vagina
with feelings of lust
also held fear and disgust.
It was for a girl
not proper to mention
all a bit forgotten
in a young girl's menstruation
passed on by generations
who had no sex education
except what they taught
one to another
the whispered pith
of smuttering myth.

I think it's fascinating
and kind of liberating
to watch this photographer
at her work
with the eyes of an artist
catching the light of a
hundred vaginas of solitude
being seen and possessed
by the women who know them best.

She makes it her mission
To shoot and to snap
Expose and disclose
give us new vision of
our precious possession

a flower that's ours
the vaginas we possess

a Regina of pleasure and tenderness
to touch and caress as part of
who WE are in body and mind.

And it's great to watch
the joy in the face
of a woman who sees her
vagina clearly
Her surprise
at the shape and the size
the folds of her labia
her clitoral crown
the shades of her skin and down.

You know each woman on tv
tells of a changing Identity.
There's a part of her
which now she can see
she says she feels different – free.
Whatever her age
whatever her background
she talks of her possession
in vision astounding
she talks of it
as something empowering
something completed and found.

Kate Collier

I. AWARENESS OF OTHERNESS

My Friend Sharon

I asked her how things were,
She sighed, then stated,
"I am exasperated by his face
Fed up with his embrace
Niggled by his bedtime wriggles
His snore is proving quite a bore
His promises seem lame
His kindness just a game
His gifts are just a way
Of getting me to stay
His smile is looking vile
His grin is not a win
His comments are banal
I've felt that for a while
His intellect really grates
We no longer feel like mates
I cannot bear his touch
We don't do it very much
I don't find him buff or fit
I'd really rather knit
I just don't find him funny
He calls me his little bunny
Which makes me feel quite sick
I don't know what makes him tick
Oh, it's really rather bleak

I've not had a very good week
He's driving me insane
Enough of me
How's you Elaine?"
She says all this, she barely stopped for air,
I think about her words and I care for my friend Sharon.
"Good grief," I say,
"You just can't stay."
"Oh no," she says, "I will not leave
I love my Steve
How dare you say such a thing?
I'm his yang and he's my ying
I thought you were my friend
Well that can easily end
If you are going to spout such hate
you'll no longer be my mate."
With that she left,
Now I'm confused,
and quite bemused,
by my friend Sharon

Liz Barnes

II. WARY OF OTHERS

Could a woman have an ego like this?

Could a woman have an ego this large?
Oversized egos can be cleaned up - several ways
I've heard there's an anti-ego spray
For the ones with an X in their pocket
busy launching another rocket
to go to a planet they own elsewhere
only to bark alone in the dark - far from here
This ego born in a 3D printer into a man flesh and blood
well we can convert him back to 2D
as a matter of world security
We could flatten his ego in Photoshop
And have some fun, pick the trimmer tool up
cut him down to size then
choose the eraser to watch his demise
His ego could shrink to a little spot
with the self-published tools of photoshop.
Who was the owner of X ?
I forgot.

Kate Collier

II. WARY OF OTHERS

Virginia

Impossible to feel another's pain, the walk to the river so easy,
cows waiting by the gate, this perfect place chalk-circled
and green as Rodmell's walls, its paintings, the pastel tiles,
the green of a Hogarth book, prints in the cottage style.

Nature is waved inside, come in, all is peaceful here,
naive and so very far from war. Bedroom sills sanatorium-green,
hysterical-green, list-green, calculation-green, war-green,
insipid spitfire-green, here to soothe and calm and colour the quiet.

Yet, for all that green - geraniums cover brick paths,
weeds in the concrete pond, grafted apple trees, primroses,
a chestnut sapling by the writing shed (leave it for now, let it grow) -
none of it is enough to stay, this kind of love, but for all that, nothing.

The Ouse is green too, a whitish sky-green;
bladderwrack waits in the brack for new salt,
fish slip down with the outgoing tide, inland gulls paddle hard
against the current and, oh, those river stones

small enough for pockets, large enough to sink the pain. A lonely place to end,
this perfect place of too much green and March an ill-timed month to die, leaves
pushing out, hellebores in flowerbeds, the borders a rush of new things
forgotten things, the worry of frost on the magnolia. But all the same

II. WARY OF OTHERS

she should've waited, held her breath, followed the sound of bleating,
watched the shepherd's bloodstained arms, a tangle of chord, a suck,
a sweep of orange membrane from the mouth,
the lungs shook clear, its mighty red cry and antidote to green.

Or ridden the train to London, slate grey rubble,
songs in the shelter to keep spirits from falling,
or slept or screamed or prayed or cried or laughed
or picked up the telephone, or something at least. Or something.

Impossible to feel another's pain - the walk to the river so easy, the sun warm,
long grass, horses grazing and birds - but all the same, she should've waited.
Seasons change, tides turn. We all should give it time:
the best and worst is still ahead, take them both together.

Nicola Garrard

II. WARY OF OTHERS

Stepping stone

The pebble in my shoe
made me limp. For years
I put up with the pain
until one day I stopped walking
altogether, kicked off the shoe
in despair. The stone came loose.
I held it in my palm, warm
where years had worn it smooth.

I tried to throw my stone
with my weak arm. I could
smash through windows
or ceilings, make a terrific mess.
But I didn't like clearing up after
plus the shards were a danger.
So I painted my stone bright colours,
sat it on the mantelpiece.

Still there was little comfort.
I put my stone in my pocket
where it weighed me down.
I thought of Virginia, and Ophelia,
and the certainty of madness.
The longer I carried my stone,
the closer it moved to the heart.
I placed my stone on the ground.

I thought it would trip me.
Instead, I found I could step taller.
It was a fine view above
the crowd. I smiled, nodded
at other heads standing
proud on their stepping stones.
Now I build my house from stone
so the wolf can't blow it down.

Ted Gooda

II. WARY OF OTHERS

The Ringmaster

He stands proud
in front of the crowd
So smart
So tall
In his suit n' all
His grin so very convincing
He brings in the clowns
with their smiles painted on
The happiness attached to them
just a con
They trip over each other
don't work together
The crowd laughs
Because they aren't very clever
Even when the poor clowns cry
No one thinks it's real
No one sees
how they try to please
 their master
He cracks the whip
 tells them to work faster
Mummy clown is dropping
spinning plates
Another juggles balls
hoping for the ringmaster to notice
She stands quietly and waits
Baby clown hesitates
before running away
But the crowd clap

when he gets her back
'Sorry,' she says
 under threat of his whip
With a very wobbly bottom lip
The show must go on
And on and on
Make up now a smear
Tracks of white tear
The crowd do not boo
they do not hiss
He sweetly blows the audience a kiss
His act approved of
How great is his reputation
God damn
He gets a standing ovation
The ringmaster accepts the applause
He bows, he is revered
This crowd don't see
how much he's feared
Then he finds his clowns
he beats them some more
The rest takes place
behind a closed door
What a circus what a show
What the ringmaster's really like
No one will ever know

Liz Barnes

II. WARY OF OTHERS

Do You Love Me?

I ask you, 'do you love me?' and you say, 'yes'
I am trying to make my brain understand this truth
It is backed up by overwhelming evidence
It is obvious, it is reality, it is a fact that you love me
But my brain fights me like Big Daddy on a Saturday afternoon
It thinks of a million reasons why this cannot be true
It backs away like it has come across a monster
Hides behind the curtains like a child at bedtime
Refuses to hear the words, claims deafness
Presents foolish stories to the contrary
Tells me not to believe you
That I am unlovable
I have been sold a lie
This is a scam, a sales technique
A woven web of deception
It runs from your words, from your 3 little words
It covers its ears
Climbs a tree
Hides underwater
Goes to sleep
Refuses to engage
Chips away at my confidence, until I am forced to ask you again
'Do you love me?'
'Yes,' you reply
But the file won't download
The piece will not slot in
The envelope does not fit
The words jar
They fade, ink faint on the page

II. WARY OF OTHERS

The book closes on itself
She loves me?
The way is blocked
The river flowing too fast to be crossed
There are closures and diversions
Until between ear and brain it gets completely lost and I have to ask you once again
'Do you love me?'
And again, you say, 'yes, I love you'
But internal whispers state this is untrue
The doubt creeps in, tiptoeing into my thoughts, stealing my objectivity
The voice will not be silenced, it is screaming at me
'SHE DOES NOT LOVE YOU'
Too loud to not hear, too believable to ignore
Why would she?
Why indeed?
It laughs at my optimism
Sneers at my naivety
Giggles at my romanticism, foolhardy, juvenile love until finally, I shout
'DO YOU REALLY LOVE ME?'
And you say,
'I will not say it again, what good are words?
I will live it every day until you are so loved your being cannot deny love's existence
Until you feel that love is the solid ground upon which you stand
Until my love has filled your soul, is brimming over, drowning you in love
Until you trust my love more than you trust yourself
Until then
Do not ask me, do I love you?
Just allow me to.'

Liz Barnes

III. MATERNAL AWARENESS

Wish You Were Here
(Blackpool Sands, Devon, 1983)

Remember Blackpool Sands
ready in swimsuits

plastic seat-burnt legs
pine hairpins to the sea

No Dogs in the car park
so stuff the spaniel

under the picnic rug
and hope for the best

quiet now, girl
something good's coming

don't bark, don't cry
more shingle than sand

pebble gems each
you'll find the best, Mum

the heart, the hole, the shell
the dog runs in, shakes

on the spread you made
oh, the quiches, the cakes
oh, Mum, wish you were here.

Nicola Garrard

III. MATERNAL AWARENESS

Little bedtime story

You breached my bedside gently, conjured
in hushed tones, slipped between sheets,
that wormed into the heart and under my skin
years before I had any say about what I wanted
to let in. Little Red Riding Hood - reveal your sin.

No. Instead we might ask Charles Perrault
and the Brothers Grimm. Let's begin
before the beginning. The title. Why not
bestow the quiet dignity of a real name? Reduced,
instead, to an item of clothing. Less. A part of a whole,

prefixed with a diminutive - least there be any doubt
Meant affectionately, they'd surely say.
But perhaps Big Red Riding Hood might
have had half a hope against a little bad wolf.
And what of red? Siren. No camouflage in the wood

so you couldn't hide. Next they weighed you
down with a heavy basket. You couldn't run.
To pile on guilt they lumbered you with duty,
caring for a bedridden grandmother. Imposed
rules, then put Eve's temptations in the way

(that old chestnut), so you'd stray. Preyed
on your good nature in befriending a sly beast.
Sent a woodcutter to the rescue. (Male, older.)
Once upon a time, I read to my daughter.
What big ears you have! I say, hoping you hear.

Ted Gooda

III. MATERNAL AWARENESS

A plea to the young unloved Mother

Warm your baby tenderly
Don't let your mother's way be yours
Hold her close to you, close, not the distance you know
from times long ago when you cried for a cuddle
out in your pram arms and legs in a muddle with
blankets off till your cries turned to screams
under the tree where no one could see.
Where feeding was timed and no one responded.

Love was scheduled to a clock. You learnt to stop.
Like a photo cropped it reduced your sense of security
Who am if they don't notice me? If they don't see me
who will I be? Keep quiet – be good like all girls should –
help your mother not to see. She's busy.
So it took you a lifetime to know your needs
numbed as you were from keeping small.
Your mother's trauma went before you. A common rule.

Hold your baby with your eyes, don't avert them with
all this crazy distraction. Or take your attention to a Whats App chat
because maybe, maybe you too are needy, just a grown-up baby,
feeling lonely, seduced from your baby by chats on your phone
because like your infant you're home alone.

Hold her close, safe, warm and connected
not the distance you know from times long ago
As she looks at you lovingly hold her tender with your eyes
so she can see she's loved and when she cries known
And please, please, please
talk to her more than your mobile phone.

Kate Collier

IV. BE AWARE

Pink

Pink Champagne
Effervescent
Given as a birthday present
Cocktails with little pink umbrellas
The glass reflecting pink dusky skies
 as girls clink and smile
flirtatiously with guys
Fizzing with joy
Straws in pink gin
Bright pink against the night
Sober no longer in sight
Pink cheeks flushed with delight
Pink fingers reach out for a hand
pink hands reach out
to help her stand
Pink blushes
at the sight of his intention
Did he fail to mention?
Pink lips moving, smiling, desiring
her pink fuddled brain
compromising
believing he must be nice

Nice like pink sugar mice
Pink stumbling
Pink fumbling
Consciousness tumbling
He takes his chance
A colourless advance
Her pink heart sinks
When she wakes and blinks

Pink memories come flooding back
Of force there was no lack
She gave no consent
in fact she cried with pink neon glo
She cried 'no!'
Now she thinks
There is no pink
She curls into a small grey ball
And cries translucent tears
 as she remembers it all.

Liz Barnes

IV. BE AWARE

Birth day

Her hair catches fire. Curls fry to copper wire
when she blows a feeble spit-filled wish
over five candles. That's when it begins.
He follows her inside the sweet shop while
she buys sugar mice. He seems nice, notices
the burnt tresses. It's her first time

alone outside home. She plays grownup though
her mother watches from the window, not ready
to cut apron strings. He's still there later, parked
outside in a van: predatory waiter. The policeman
brings bewildering conversations about strangers
she can't reconcile with respecting elders. She's done

wrong, it seems, because it changes everything.
Her hair is scissored into a shiny pageboy trim.
Paul Bailey draws diagrams on the school desk
of how babies are made. It sounds like poppycock.
On the way to school, something in the bushes.
Rustlings, sharp intake of breath, flash of pale flesh.

She thinks at first he must be in some distress, before
the rude sting of understanding. Years pass. She takes
matters into her own hands: red streaks, punk-dyed.
The next jeans-down clown freak taps with flashlight
on the glass window pane at midnight. She screams
alone in the all-female, off-campus student halls.

IV. BE AWARE

A magnet for this sort of thing, unfortunately.
The fed sighs. Such a fuss. He was only outside looking
in, after all. No harm done. All sorts of cuts after that.
Loose waves, bleach-blonde, cropped, bobbed, shaved.
It doesn't matter. She still loses count of the violating.
Look, don't touch, she wills her hair to say.

Grey-haired, she trades her plaits for venomous asps.
She makes a wish. Nothing has been extinguished.
Now girl turned crone can spit, burn, turn them to stone.

Ted Gooda

IV. BE AWARE

Cot Poems

1
He kept her locked in a parakeet's cage
All night she screeched and squealed
Covered her eyes and couldn't see
A baby shouldn't know such things
A baby shouldn't know.
She froze as she felt her keeper's hands
Froze in her tender young soul
He had the key to her freedom
but by day she flew beyond
to a land of infant magic
where a spark of light could be found.
No-one protected her from the dark.

2
Her father echoed her sobbing sound
It was dropped in the curve of a wave
Thrust and thrown and churned around
Stranded in a far off bay.
She searched in every woven shell
scattered near and far
The echo she has never found
lost in the tidal draw
One day for another to understand
but never be known by her.

3
She knows it now this secret kept
It liberates her soul
And she can find her voice again,
no muffled sound or tightened throat
no retching, spewing, giving in
her breath no longer held.
Her eyes no longer screwed up tight
It's here, here she affirms the baby in her
who lived a fraternal hell.

Kate Collier

V. BEWARE

Birch Syrup

I dreamed of you last night;
you came into my dream, sorry-feeling and quiet
and watched me tap my birches.
You saw my penknife draw a nick in the white bark,
bleed clear sap into a bottle
and sometimes over my tongue, a drink of spring.
I wanted to boil it down until thick,
bottle it for your porridge. I wondered how long it would take.
I wondered if the cut would ever heal.
I wondered what we can ever give without reducing another.
I wondered if you'd accept
this stolen tree sweet, this scrumped blood of the wood.

Nicola Garrard

V. BEWARE

Breast Work

They were all on the beach
with the leader in reach
And I went up to him said
I hear you do breast work, can I join in?
I need my boobs enhancing.

He said breast work
not a bit of it
you've got the wrong end of the stick
I'm afraid we don't do tits

It's breath work we do
Inflate our chests
lung exercise, not increase your size
And pictures of breast pumps come to mind
Blood pressure machines all dancing in time
Waves that ripple and frozen nipples
Breaths and breasts and 34D
maybe now more a C or B

And in our dry robes in meditative rapture
quizzical seals out in the water
capture our weekly 8am sutra
they have no need of a camera.

We all count our in-breath and then are out
to the rhythm of a boom box that drowns the sea
In and out and the space between where
there's all that room to expire completely.

And it's there in that place
where I'm shivering and blue
that my breasts deflate to a 32!

Kate Collier

V. BEWARE

What a Shame

Perfect nails, perfect hair, eyebrows perfect pair
Mind got skewed as she looked in the mirror
No love, no glimmer, just wishes she was slimmer
Self-hate no debate, in fact, it's a family trait
Compliments on screen, but some are mean
They stick as she flicks over the page her stage
Words hurt, call her dirty, ugly, fat, chop off your head you'd be better off dead
One guy starts to chat, says, 'you ain't all that but let's see you without that top'
She types stop
But she lies in bed at night knows he's right, she'll do it and maybe he'll be her man.
She's got a plan, post a picture #wantsex, webcam on she sends a text
He replies, let's see your breasts,' then says; 'I wanna see the rest'
Her ego stroked, she feels real stoked, she strikes a pose
Image he posts and boasts that she's his girl
Her tits are hits with his mates, they rate her high, he says they're going out
She pouts, but doubts, doesn't want do today but must obey or he'll say goodbye
She gives the pics, he saves the clips and sends them round the world
They'll never disappear let's be clear when she's old and wise she'll despise the things she did but she won't ever get rid
Potential bosses giggle as she wriggles in her chair
They say no because of what they see for free
They frown she says she can't take them down
She begs them to be kind, but they think she's dirty, far too flirty
A big grey cloud that follows her around
If only she could go back in time, tell herself she's fine and help her love herself
What she wouldn't give to live that time again with her head screwed on
He'd be gone, no threats, regrets or shame
What a shame

Liz Barnes

V. BEWARE

Banishing the branks

In the meeting he
manipulates my meaning,
unlistening   until my words dry.
I let him. We connive
in twisting the quieting knife.

I command my body to obey,
am betrayed
by water from my eyes,
because he has
centuries on his side. I know

it looks like weakness yet I feel
anything but meek. In spite
of this   I'm silenced.
The bit stops my tongue
just as surely as if I'm locked

securely in branks. Shamed,
aggrieved as my Tudor sisters
must have been, I wonder why
this punishment is kept only
for women's abasement. Today

is one too many times
he's undermined and smiled.
Civilised   torture
shapes my spirit stronger.
I scream inside

V. BEWARE

until the world around me
capsizes. And every tear
which slides down
past that iron cage
finds its way to the river

of rage flowing through ancient veins.
And even as I cry I feel strength
well up inside   and rise   and rise.
Soon I'll burst my banks to smash
my way out of the branks.

Ted Gooda

V. BEWARE

Step Forward in Solidarity

Step forward in solidarity
for her, for she, for them, for me.
I will be heard..
I will be seen:
my body, my voice, my choice,
not oppressed,
not second best.
Real equality.
We must step forward

Step forward in solidarity
towards a world
we desire.
Women of every age
will fuel the raging fire,
will insist society turn the page
to the chapter where, finally,
we have our say,
speak our minds every day,
in every town and city.
We don't want your pity,
we want forward motion,
will cause a commotion
because, in every venue,
it's overdue.
That the female version
makes an assertion
that her talent is out there,
we must not care to be shy.
Timid must fly away, so we may
showcase everything we have to give.

Step forward in solidarity
and live differently.
Believe in yourself,
care for your health,
your body,
your wealth.
No duplicity,
just authenticity.

Step forward in solidarity
Not back
Don't take any flack
Look ahead
Speak out
Shout!

Step forward in solidarity
Your message is yours
This cause belongs to us all
For those not physically able
We give them our hand
In your heart you can stand

You can step forward in solidarity
Show us what you've got
Put your bit in the pot
We must work together
Sever submission
Commission your sister, your friend,
your mother
Find another to step forward with
Give yourself permission
I call on you to stand together

V. BEWARE

To step forward in solidarity
There is no one and nothing that can stop you
Can stop your forward movement
Your beautiful soul
Be brave, hang onto your goal
You are perfect
Don't have an unreal expectation
Of who or how you should be
Just be yourself, be free

Step forward in solidarity
For every woman in history
Who has suffered through the years
Whose lives will not be in vain
Because we will honour their pain
Refuse to accept those who try to shame them
Even blame them
Silence them
Take the power from those who committed violence against them

Step forward in solidarity
We say
No more
Rich or poor
In solidarity we step forward
Toward a better world for us
For us all
Join the fight
Black or white
With intention and motivation
With truth and clarity
We will step forward in solidarity!

Liz Barnes

Thanks are due to the editors and publishers who first selected these poems:

'What a shame' & 'Do you love me?' were published in *A Little Bit of Pain and a Whole Lot of Love*, 2022, The Real Press

'My Friend Sharon' was published in *I Swallowed the World*, 2023, The Real Press

'Cot Poems' was published in *Cocktail Bitter and Sweet*, 2021, The Real Press

'Virginia' was published in *Frogmore Papers*, 2024

'Birch Syrup' was published in *The IRON Book of Tree Poetry*, IRON Press, 2020.

'The difference between boys and girls' was published in Vole Books Summer Anthology 2023 *Washed with Noon*

'Stepping stone' was published by Vole Books Anthology 2023 *Poetry is not Dead*

'Birth day' was published by *Wildfire Words*, 2024

'Banishing the branks' was published in *Silence & Selvedge*, Earthy Little Acorns Poetry Press, 2024